Quilting 101
Beginners

Your start to finish guide
on quilting

NATASHA BENNINGFIELD

Contents

Introduction

AS PEOPLE HAVE STARTED LOOKING for ways to simplify their lives and cut back on technology, many old crafts and hobbies have begun to gain attention and popularity. Among these revived hobbies are sewing, knitting, crocheting, and quilting.

If you know how to sew, you can make and repair your own clothes. If you can knit and crochet, you can make your own presents, decor, and gifts for close friends and family members. But what exactly do you do with a quilt? If you have a blanket, is there really a need to quilt another? Furthermore where did quilting come from?

When you think about today's use of quilting, it can really seem like an out of place hobby. People that are die hard quilters tend to have too many quilts, way more than they would ever reasonably need; and, they are constantly finding excuses to give them away. Doesn't this seem like a bit of a waste? Absolutely not!

While quilters today may have a hard time finding excuses to claim their hobby as a necessity there is still a real need for the task, and it isn't new. Archaeologists and historians have been able to unearth examples and evidence of quilts back to 3400 BC, the time of the Egyptian first dynasty. In ancient China, between the time period of 1st century BC and 2nd century AD, there is evidence of quilting.

In the 11th century in Europe, knights wore quilted undergarments for protection. This concept eventually grew to women wearing quilted petticoats. These early examples of quilt usages were first for warmth. They had all the elements of a quilt: two layers of cloth, installation of fiber in between, with stitching to hold the insulating fiber in place from shifting. These same four elements of a quilt are found in present day quilts too.

The ancient quilted undergarments evolved to coverings for the bed as well as to the wall for warmth and insulation. Quilts also became family heirlooms, being passed down to future generations. In wills and estate planning, quilts became a part of a person's furnishings to be given away. They had value. Quilts also had status. If you came from wealth and affluence, quilts were generally bought using high grade quality textiles and fabrics. No doubt the stitching would have been more intricate too.

While those from lesser money and wealth still had need of quilts, they were likely to be made from old scraps and old worn clothes that had outlived their usefulness.

Back then, fabrics were a commodity that no one wanted to waste. They didn't have Goodwills and thrift stores to leave their unwanted clothes at for tax write-off abilities. No, instead, they simply recycled.

Quilting was also seen as a family pass time that the females joined together for. While doing this activity together, they could gossip, share feelings, and essentially be there for one another on something that would mean a lot to everyone involved.

This activity came to America with the first settlers. Back then, they were still used for warmth, but also as a form of currency. Present day quilts are seen as a marker of the creator's time.

During the civil war in America, quilts were made to raise money and to help keep the soldiers warm during the winter months. At the time of the underground railroad, there have been stories of how quilts were used to indicate certain homes and places for runaway slaves to hideout. Many of the patterns that come with quilt making are so popular because of their historical origins and importance of the past.

Quilts are still seen as necessary items during cold, winter months. They're also seen as a growing industry with lots of potential as artistic outlets, and a business. Many hard working individuals have started to delve into the world of quilt making for pure, personal enjoyment only to have it blossom into something profitable.

Although many a quilter's interest might have begun as something innocent, in a way to simply pass down time, or relieve stress, has often turned into designing patterns, writing books, and developing new techniques.

There are actually quilt celebrities, who are widely known in quilting circles, whose ways of manipulating the fabric, fiber, and material of the quilt is seen as an art medium that many find simply amazing. With the money, artistic talent, and experience found within quilting circles, it can all be very intimidating for the interested novice.

The point of this book is to cut through that intimidation, and bring you down to the basics of quilting: The building blocks of the trade. Once you know and understand the basics, you will be able to put the touch of quilting in numerous types of handmade products that can help distinguish your personal touch from another's. '

I'll finish this book with a step-by-step quick guide to getting started on hand quilting and machine quilting. Of course, to follow along more closely, you'll want to get your hands on a simple quilt pattern. A simple "Google" search should return back several freebies to get you started with. Just think small, like a baby blanket. And now, without further ado, let's learn about the quilt!

Basic Tools Must-Haves

YOU REALLY DON'T NEED a lot of tools and equipment to get started making your first quilt. However, just like any favorite past time hobby or craft, there are a lot of non-essential items that can make your work easier, more enjoyable, and quicker to finish. Everybody loves a project they can finish in a reasonable amount of time!

Still, just the idea of all the tools available to begin your quilting project, can be so overwhelming you can freeze from simply not knowing where to start. I don't want you to be overwhelmed. Instead, I want you to understand what it is you need at a bare minimum to get started.

I also want to provide you with the information needed to make informed decisions regarding other basic tools that will help you complete the job as well. You will quickly discover that there are non-essential tools that you will decide you simply can't quilt without. Use your best judgment, and let your budget really decide what you need.

Remember, tools and equipment are not the only things you'll need to buy to start quilting. You will also need the following:

Quilt Top: Usually patchwork-pieced, appliqued, or a piece of whole cloth (rare)

Backing: This is the bottom layer of your quilt. It can be one piece, or partially piece (a new technique) or patchwork-piece for reversibility.

Binding: A strip of fabric that closes off the raw edges of the quilt.

Keep these needs in mind while you make your list of equipment needed to get started. Below, I've written out a list of items you simply must have initially.

The bare minimum

To get started quilting, less than 5 tools are really needed. If you know even a bit about clothing, I am sure that you can get them easily. Do you know what they are? Needles, shears or scissors, pens, rulers, and marking tools. Let's see how you'll use these with your quilts.

Needles

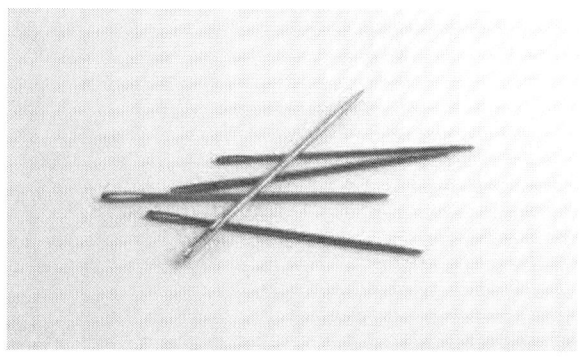

That's right, plain hand sewing needles. They can be purchased in packages of only one size or in a variety of sizes. What you need will depend on what you plan on using to hold your quilt together. For many projects, however, regular hand sewing needle will do. For others you might want a tapestry needle if you are planning on using yawn, or some other thick thread, for topstitching.

Needles come in sizes ranging from number 1 through 12 they are also categorized as being either sharks or between. Sharps are generally the all-purpose needle that is used for applique and piercing fabrics. Betweens are what you will need for quilting. The higher you get on the number range for needles the finer and shorter you will need a will be. For quilting, you will want a range between 7 and 12.

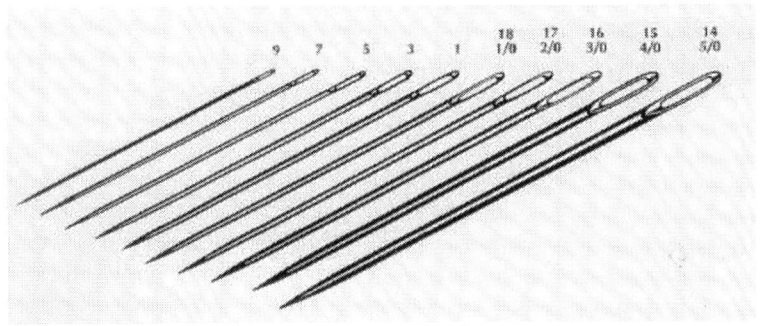

Shears or scissors

There is no doubt that you will absolutely need to have a pair of sharp fabric cutting scissors. This means that they are not your go-to scissors when you need to open up a bag of chicken tenders, or you need to pierce the frozen bag of veggies. These scissors will be specifically used for quilting.

Make sure that you can hold your scissors or with a steady hand. If you go with the pair of shears, they will have a smaller hole for your fingers, but then a large hole for several singers to fit in. Shears also have bent handles so that they can slide easily along a flat surface while you cut.

If you are not used to shears, they can be a bit tricky to get the hang of. Personally, I prefer scissors over shears because shears are difficult for me to handle. Scissors are typically used for small areas to trim down, and for cutting through excess fabric. Shears are used generally for large cutting jobs such as patchwork pieces.

You will also need a good pair of scissors reserved specifically for paper cutting. This is because when you follow two patterns for your templates quilts, you will be cutting templates out of plastic and or cardboard. For this reason your scissors must be sharp. You will probably replace your paper cutting scissors more frequently and a lot more often than you will replace your fabric cutting shears or scissors.

Pins

This is essential for your starting tools because you will need something to hold your fabric layers in place before sewing them together. And of course, to make things more difficult, there are several types of pins available.

For quilting, you're going to want long, thin straight pins. However any type of pen will do if it is what you have on hand at the moment and are pressed with your budget. Long, thin pins are better because they will not leave a large hole in your fabric. Plus they will be easier to stick in and pull out while you are sleeping with the machine or with your hands.

Safety pins

1" number one safety pins can also be used to hold your fabrics together before you start to machine quilt. They are also extremely useful for pinning on applique motifs to top your project off. However, these are just a matter of preference, as you could really get by with just some regular pins.

Thimbles

Do people still use these? Absolutely! Thimbles are *necessary* for hand sewing. Modern day thimbles are made to fit on any finger of your hand that you want. They protect your fingers from the pokes of the needle while quilting, and can even help you pierce the fabric easier for sewing too.

While sewing, your stitches will need to go through all layers of the fabric, including the batting. For this reason, many quilters view them as a necessity. Thimbles are not easy to get accustomed too. In fact it might make your work a little slower at first. However, you will find that with time, you will feel like you cannot sew without one.

They come in a variety of sizes for your fingers, and also in different types of material: metal, silver, gold, plastic, leather and more.

Bias bars

This piece of equipment is perfect for making narrow pieces of fabric strips. Bias bars, also known as Celtic bars, make the job of making a narrow strip of fabric super easy.

Bias bars are small, metal bars that come in a variety of sizes. You use them by following the directions to cut your fabric to the proper length and width. Once that is completed, you'll use a sewing machine to sew the fabric together with the proper seam allowance of about an eighth of an inch. Once you have sewn together your small strip of fabric, you'll insert the bias bar into the fabric.

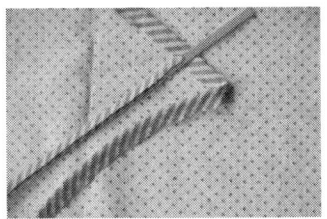

Center the seam allowance in the middle of the bias strip, and then press with your iron. Afterwards you can take the bar out. The result is a nice, long pressed strip that can be used for stems on patchwork or applique, or as bag straps, spaghetti straps, and things of that nature. However, for quilting, bias cars are used mainly for stims, and other types of applique work. Look at the following quilt design. Those are bias bars in their glory. Now you know why they're also called Celtic bars too!

Rotary Cutters

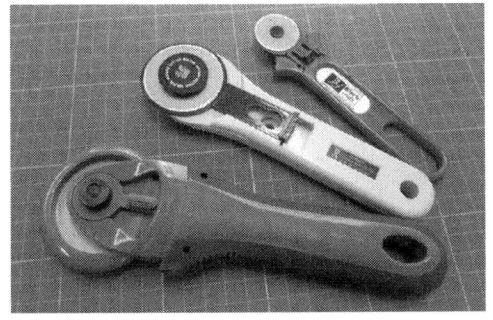

A rotary cutter, or circular blade, is perfect for cutting fabric strips. It is also pretty effective for cutting out other shapes and patterns too. They save cutting time and really make it easy for you to cut out your design. Some people complain that cutting with shears for their hands. A rotary cutter often helps.

If you plan to use a rotary cutter, you will need a mat that has been designed specifically to withstand the use of the cutter. That means it must have a self-healing surface. The special mat will allow the cutter to cut on it without leaving ridges and damaging the cutter the next time you need use it.

Rotary cutting mats come in different sizes, some as small as a six inch square and others as large as a whole table. Smaller mats obviously store better and they are great for taking to a class if you need a cutting mat. However, larger mats require a lot of room to store properly. Very large mats are expensive; they can come with the ability to lay flat even after being rolled for long period of time.

Do should not iron on your cutting mat. It is likely to be some mixture of silicone and plastic, and the heat will only warp it. Use extra caution when you're using rotary cutters. Always cut going away from your body by keeping your hand on the cutting board and away from the blade.

When you are done cutting, make sure the blade is completely sheathed and locked in place. Always make sure that when you are not cutting, the blade is retracted, and locked to prevent accidents. Also, make sure your cutter is where small children cannot even see it or reach it. Once an accident has happened, it can't be undone.

Rulers

A plastic see through quilting ruler is necessary for cutting templates. These rulers are often used with the mat and a rotary cutter. Having never quoted before, it can be difficult for you to determine what your specific preference will be. Get advice from other seasoned quilters and your local shop if you can before making a purchase.

One trick that I use, since I tend to use a particular width of strip on a regular basis, is a metal strip that has been cut to the width of the common size I need. An example of this would be whether or not you like to make log cabin quilts:

These types of quilts tend to use 1½ inch strips. You can purchase metal templates in this size. Doing this eliminates the need to constantly measure using a see-through ruler for accuracy while you cut.

I prefer the metal strip because when you are using a ruler, it is easy to use the wrong guidance. If you are cutting many strips of the same length and width, lessen your chance of making a mistake by using the first strip that you have measured as a guide. Pin it down and use it to measure the other strips as needed.

Clear rulers also tend to slip and slide on fabric. This will make cutting pretty frustrating, as I'm sure you can imagine. Because of this, a company ingeniously made small adhesive sandpaper pieces to put on the back of your ruler in order to keep it from slipping on the fabric while you cut.

They also have sandpaper backed metal strips for the same reason. I do not recommend using sandpaper backed measuring guides on delicate fabrics, for obvious reasons. The sandpaper will snag your fabric, pulling the threads.

Templates

Back in the day, old women used whatever they could find to make templates for cutting. They generally used light cardboard. However, plastic templates have solved every issue that cardboard templates created. The problem with cardboard is that after a while, and after a frequent use, the edges wear, curl, and distort. Accuracy becomes impossible.

Plastic templates get rid of that issue. Also with a plastic template, they can come with or without graph lines, rough or smooth on one side, clear, colored, or opaque. They can also come with non-melting abilities for when you need to press on applique. And they also come in multiple different sizes. Plastic pre-cut templates are really useful.

Regardless of whether or not you are going to use homemade templates made from cereal boxes, shoe boxes, tissue boxes, or if you bought them in a store, you should make sure to mark them. Find a way to distinguish your templates so that you will be able to keep the pattern throughout your project.

Marking tools

A regular pencil is not going to be enough. A way to mark your fabric, appliques, or templates is necessary because a different type of marking tool is required for different quilting-making tasks.

When marking your template to cut, you will need a very fine pencil. This can be satisfied using a constantly sharpened number 2 lead pencil, or a 0.5mm mechanical pencil. This is because you don't want errors while you cut. Thicker ways of tracing, or marking leave a line that is too big to know where you should actually be cutting. If your line is too thick, you will have an inaccurate cut out.

Some quilters do not care what they are using to mark out the template for their project. That is because most quilters usually make their mark on the wrong side of the fabric. If you fall into one of these categories, just make sure you are careful of the pen that you are using. Light colored thread can pick up color from the ink you used to mark your template.

Some of the options you have are silver drawing pencils or white chalk pencils. Many quilters also like wash out markers. However, other quilters might not recommend wash out markers. While the color may wash out when your product is complete, chemicals may still remain in the fabric that can cause discoloration and fabric integrity loss over time.

Tool Kit Add-ons

WITH ANY SORT OF NEW hobby or craft, there will always be a list of tools that are absolutely necessary, and then a list of tools that you might like to have, but don't need, as well as a list of tools that you definitely want. This chapter is dedicated to those tools in the last two types of categories.

These tools have been designed to make your life easier. The will also make your project that much more professional. Investing time into some of these products will more than likely help you finish your project sooner.

Let's take a look at what tools can make your quilting easier:

Frames and Hoops

The purpose of a frame or hoop is to help make your job quilting all the more easier. This is why it's a tool kit add on. You don't really need it—although many quilters will beg to differ! If you're interested in one of these to begin your quilting project, consider the following information first:

Most present-day quilters prefer a small hoop over a large floor frame. This is mainly because of the practical nature of the hoop. You can sit in a chair and still have easy access to the patch you're working on.

Floor frames are not only expensive, but they take up a lot of room to. Frames and hoops are available in a variety of sizes and shapes. You can buy them for as little as $5 or $10 to as much as $400 or more. With all these options, it will no doubt be hard for you to determine whether or not you really need one.

Getting started, it is definitely something you can do without. If you're interested in getting one to begin with, though, I would suggest that you get some advice from an experienced quilter. Attempt to borrow different types of hoops or frames before making a purchase.

Every quilter has a different and more preferred way to do things. What works for one person, isn't necessarily going to work for you. Keep yourself from spending too much money on items you only think you need. If you can, experiment when possible by borrowing certain items so that you know what works best for you.

Pressing equipment

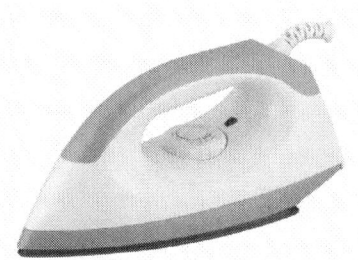

While you quilt, you are going to require something to press out your pieces. A good household iron is sufficient. Some quilt makers find themselves unable to recommend a steam press as it can stretch pieces of your fabric out of shape. If you stick with cotton, a steam iron will be fine. Just consider the fabrics you're using for your quilt.

Once you've chosen your iron, take care of it. Clean it often so that your fabric is not destroyed by buildup and residue. Build up is likely to happen from iron on interfacing, fusibles, and other materials. I recommend that after you are finished ironing with each of these types of appliques, that you thoroughly and completely clean your iron.

Commercial solutions are available for this. Make sure that you do not use abrasive cleaners, as they can fill the steam holes and deposit the chemicals onto your fabrics later. Ensure the long life of your iron by reading the instructions that recommend cleaning products.

Avoid water from your tap to put in the water tank because it contains chemicals and minerals that can build up on the inside and outside of the iron. This can leave residue and markings on your fabric or finished pieces. Overtime, leaving water in your iron can cause rusting. Instead, get into the habit of using distilled water to protect your iron and your fabric.

Fabric & Batting

THERE ARE A LOT OF DIFFERENT options when it comes to choosing your fabrics. 100% cotton is recommended for most quilts, if not all.. This is because cotton fabrics crease easily during the pressing stage, they absorb moisture, are durable, and don't easily wear. Blends not quite so easy. They do not press easily, and are a little more difficult to use in patchwork. However, blends don't fade as easily as cotton; they also don't lay the same way.

If you like working with scrap patchwork, the combined fabrics of different types are likely to come in a variety of fabric types. It all depends on the quilt. Old quilts tend to be very special, using silk, wool, and cotton. Combining fabric like this requires special care and knowledge of what you're doing. As you know, some fabrics are more fragile than others; and, combining them as such will mean a different way to get them clean.

Buying fabrics

Some fabrics have a directional print. This means that you will want to cut them a certain way in order to get to the image on the fabric. Using these types of fabrics in your quilt requires additional length because of the special cutting specifications that are necessary.

If you are going with print fabric, then the scale is important. If the print is too large, and it has to be cut into very small pieces, the design will be lost overall. Keep this in mind while you're purchasing fabrics. Examine the print, and think about how it will look when its cut into smaller patches. Think about whether or not the color will be lost, or whether or not the motive for disappear when cut.

You will find that every quilt pattern you come across will have a list of materials so that you can recreate exactly as it is shown. However, you don't have to follow the fabric exactly if you have a stash of fabric with you. Most experienced quilters tend to purchase fabrics in their preferred amounts. Use the following guidelines if you are just getting started:

- 1/4 yard if you just want to have that pattern in your collection
- 1 yard do you really like the pattern of the fabric and expect to use it more than just a little
- 3 yards if you know for sure you will use it in a quilt
- 5 to 6 yards if you plan to have it at backing

- If you are interested in making scrap quilts, consider the fact that many shops sell a quarter yard piece, fat quarters (18" x 22"), or a fat eights (9" x 18").

Color

When looking at your quilting patterns, it is likely that you will see different colors that you would like to see the pattern in. This is perfectly fine. Mini scrap designs for quotes rely heavily on the contrast of the values then on the pre-planned, coordinated colors in the pattern.

Getting started, I recommend that you just look at a large number of completed quilts. Your feelings and thoughts concerning the colors used will help you understand what you are looking for when it comes to quilt designs and patterns.

Preparing the fabric for use

There are quite a few different opinions regarding prewashing fabric. Some quilters pre wash as soon as they buy them. Others do not wash the fabric at all.

There really is no right or wrong way. However, there are really only two reasons to wash your fabric before you use. The first reason is that it might shrink. Good quality fabrics are already preshrunk and don't shrink much when they are washed.

The second reason is to determine whether or not the fabric is colorfast. Still, prewashing fabric is not a guarantee that it will not run the next time it is washed. Even when an experienced quilter will tell you to do vinegar and salt water rinses, it only prevent color from running during that wash, not in subsequent washes. The vinegar and salt water home remedy is something you will have to repeat every time you want to wash your finished quilt.

Rinsing your fabric until the water runs clear will not ensure that your fabric will not run later either. Instead, it only pulls die from the fabric, dulling the colors. Using harsh detergents will only draw more die out as well.

If you are set on prewashing your fabric, make sure to use a mild soap, especially for quilts, and very old fabrics. You don't want to ruin the fabric needed in your quilt. If you are interested in machine quilting, you should know that many quilters of this type do not prewash their fabrics. The stiffness from the unwashed fabric creates an easier time for machine piercing; and, the shrinkage that can occur after you wash a finished quilt can actually help hide the machine quilting stitches.

If you decide not to prewash your fabric, but you are still concerned about your fabric running, you should test the color fastness of the darkest fabric with your lightest piece in the quilt. Do this by washing a small piece of the both fabrics using a mild detergent. Use the detergent you plan to wash the entire quilt with. Furthermore, let the two pieces dry on top of the other. If the darkest color does not run, you can be confident about using them before prewashing. On the other hand, if it does run, you might want to reconsider your colors.

Fabric grain

It is important to understand the grain and what your fabric has. Fabrics are put together using threads in a crosswise and lengthwise direction. In other words, the threads crisscross. The threads cross at right angles. The more threads you have per inch, the stronger the fabric will be.

The crosswise threads, or grain, will have a bit of give. They will be able to stretch a little. Lengthwise threads will not stretch at all. When you cut your fabric at a 45 degree angle to the crosswise and lengthwise grains, you make a bias edge. Bias edges stretch a whole lot more when pulled.

It is important for you to understand this because templates will mark this grain. When you use a template, grain lines will be marked with arrows on certain patterns. These arrows are marked to indicate how the template needs to be cut in relation to the grain.

The arrow should be placed to run on one thread. It will not be necessary for you to find an exact match, but it is important to place the arrow on the marked template with one long lengthwise grain in your fabric.

Thread

Luckily, you really don't have to put much thought into thread. Plain cotton, or cotton covered polyester, is perfect for most pieces. Inexpensive polyester grades are not recommended because they can damage the fibers and the cotton fabric of your quilt.

You should always buy the best quality thread you can find. Lesser quality cotton threads have a tendency to create a lot of lent. This is especially true of machine sewing. If you are machine quilting, the lent can gather within the machines moving parts and cause you issues later. Also, getting lesser quality threads can cause your product to not be as durable. Your thread is likely to snap, or break in the near future.

When you pull out the seams of your quilt, you should not be able to see your thread. You can use a different type of thread for when you piece your top together, but many experienced quilters prefer a different thread for piecing, and then a thread for quilting the layers together. If using piecing thread for quilting thread, you will need to wax it to keep them from tangling with the piecing thread while you quilt. I personally suggest quilting thread as it reduces any tangling.

There are more types of thread, but for a beginner, you can get by with cotton or cotton covered polyester for your piecing, and quilting thread. Specialty thread, like rayon, is best for machine sewing. Also, it adds a nice lustrous shine to your stitches. For hand applique, you should use colors that match and blend with the piece you are going sewing. That can often means changing threads often!

Another tip: Do not use quilting thread for machine quilting unless specified for such usage. Nylon monofilament thread has been recommended for machine quilting. Metallic threads can be used for hand quilting, but I do not recommend it because they have been known to break while stitching. However, improvements have been made to prevent that breakage. They do work well when made for such in machine quilting projects. Again, specialty threads are usually preferred for the luster they can bring to your project.

Batting

A quilt consists of backing, the top piece, and then the batting. Batting is the material you plan to use to give your quilt thickness, warm, or loft. The warmth of your quilt will be determined by the thickness, in fiber type. For example, if you choose to use a batting a down feathers, they will hold air longer and we'll be great, excellent insulators. Some people prefer silk, cotton, or wool to down feathers, because they are insulate well too.

Cotton is a very good first batting to work with. However, they require very close quilting lines of 1 ½" or closer in order to prevent scrunching and lumping, especially after laundry.

Working with natural fibers might be a bit difficult, as they are more expensive than cotton or polyester batting. If you choose to work with them, be aware that it requires special techniques. It is not advised for beginners. Polyester batting is very inexpensive to work with because of how polyester is made, your quilting lines can be further apart than cotton.

Preparing to Quilt

FOR YOUR FIRST QUILT, you should start easy, something small. A baby quilt is just the thing. If you know how many blocks you want, then you should determine how many pieces of fabric you will use. In this tutorial, I have chosen to use 16 blocks, or 16 different pieces of fabric. You can choose the same, or 8, repeating the first set of blocks.

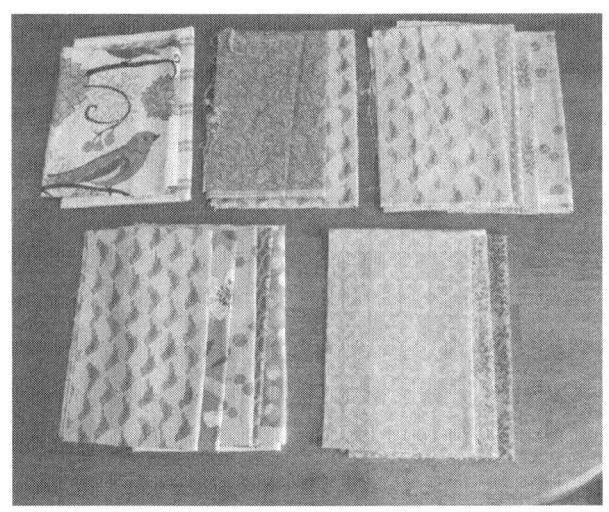

If you are not planning on applying much applique, or doing much patchwork, then you will want to use fabric that has nice prints on it. The print will do the design for you.

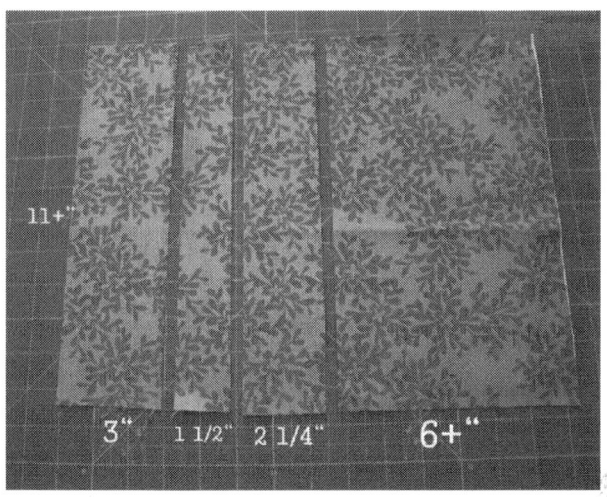

For the quilt top, begin by making your top pieces. Follow the design for your specific quilt. For this tutorial the design consist sof blocks made from the following strip sizes 3", 1 ½", 2 ¼", and 6+". The + is to allow for room during sewing (if you struggle keeping a good seam allowance). You'll want room to "square off" the blocks before piecing the top layer together.

It might help you to lay out your blocks in the pattern you will want them stitched in. You will take each block to the sewing machine to begin sewing the strips together to make your solid block.

When you begin sewing your top piece together, strive for a constant seam allowance. I prefer to use ¼". When you are finished with the blocks for your top piece, press the seams flat.

Square off the edges to create the final pieces to be sewn together.

Place the pieces of your top layer together. Pin the edges together at the corners. Once your quilt top is pinned together, add it with your batting and backing, and you can begin quilting in a fashion that you like.

Hoop Quilting

Don't make the mistake of viewing the hoops as a type of embroidery hoop. Your quilt should not be tight or taut, but loose. Place one hoop beneath the backing of the quilt, and the other on top. Push down until it's flush.

Quilting techniques include "in the ditch" (along the seams) or "overall" (over the seams and across the pattern). Overall is typically completed using a sewing machine. When ditch stitching, many quilters prefer to outline shapes and ojects in the top layer.

Machine Quilting

A SEWING MACHINE IS NECESSARY for piecing a quilt top together and for machine quilting. While machine quilting can be a fast and effective way to complete your project in a timely manner, it also means you are going to need a different set of tools, and to follow a different set of guidelines for your project.

If you do not plan to do much hand sewing, but you purchased a machine specifically for quilting, then you will need to know what type of sewing machine needle is required. The size of the needle that you will need for your quilt will be determined by the type of fabric you will sew with, as well as the type of thread that you will be using. Reading the sewing machine manual can give you some suggestions and information specific to your machine. What I am going to tell you will be helpful too.

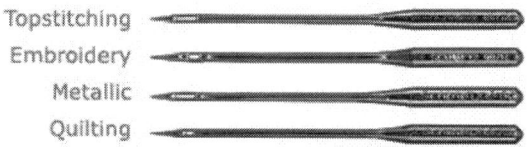

The standard sewing machine needles are generally the #80/20 needle. At least a #90/14 needle is what your machine will require for heavier fabrics. If your needle is not strong enough to handle the tension created from sewing, it can break. Also your needle may have difficulty piercing your fabric if not using the right type.

Just regular hand quilting has different techniques, machine quilting has different techniques that will require a different type of pressure foot, as well as different machine settings. Consider the following information very carefully.

When you're ready to start quilting with your machine, you can actually piece the majority your quilt together with pins. If you've done this, you'll have to remove the safety pins as you approach them while you sew. Do not try to stay over a safety pin. Sewing over a pin can make them extremely difficult to remove later; it is extremely dangerous, as it can easily break your needle. If your needle is broken, you put yourself at danger because you can easily send a needle fragment right into your eye!

Personally, I feel that machine quilting is best for preparing the top layer of your quilt. Think about a large size object. Triangles, circles, four squares. Still, there are a group of cultures out there who prefer the sewing machine for an entire quilting project. If you think you might be leaning more towards this idea, because hand quilting doesn't appeal to you, make sure that you have adequate space to the rear and the left of your machine in order to support the weight of the quilt.

If your quilt is not properly supported, the fabric can pull your machine right off the table and onto the floor. It can also make sewing in the right groove for your pattern difficult.

For a quilt that is larger than a 36" x 36" square, you will need to prepare it for quilting it in the following way:

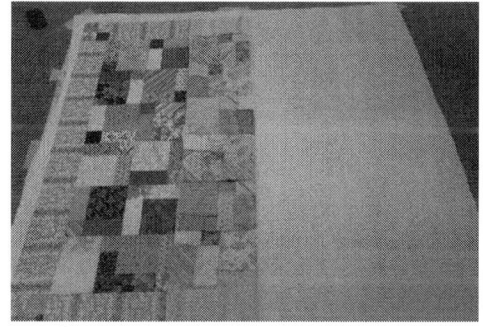

Put the basted quilt (top later, batting, and backing secured temporarily with pins, clips, or temporary spray on adhesive) on the floor and roll the two ends towards the center. Keep a good sized square available in the center.

This is where you will begin quilting. You can secure the rolls with safety pins.

You can also secure the rolls with bicycle clips. You can find these special types of fasteners from a sporting goods store. They are even carried at some sewing or quilting stores. Bicycle clips are designed to hold your pants leg against your body while cycling so that they are not caught in the bicycle chain. Because of their flexibility in with the tiny hole for clipping, it makes them double as a great way to keep your basted quilt rolled and prepped for machine quilting.

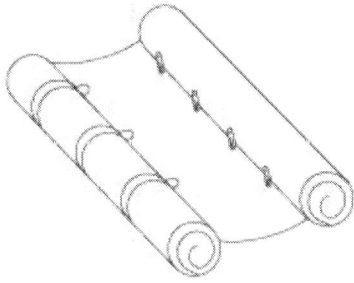

Once your large project is prepared and rolled and secured evenly in place, you will need to determine how you will sew it together. Being a beginner, I must recommend that you use a straight line for quilting.

Straight line is the easiest and quickest form of machine quilting available. Your results will always be good! What you need is an even feed presser foot.

In the above picture, a regular foot is the right, and the even feed is to the left. These type of pressure feet are also called walking feet. If your machine does not come with one, you will need to go to a sewing center in order to buy one. Before you go however, make sure you check with your machine's manual so that the store clerk can help you find the correct one for your machine model.

An even feed pressure foot is required for machine quilting so that the fabric will be smooth, and pucker free.

The even feed foot is able to pull all the layers of your quilt to the machine evenly. If you attempt to machine quilt without it the feed dogs, the teeth beneath the needle that help grab the fabric, will only feed the bottom layer of fabric through the machine. The batting and the top players will be vulnerable to puckering because they are not being fed to the machine at the same rate as the bottom layer. You will need to get aquatinted with your machine before you can start machine quilting:

1. Threading your machine

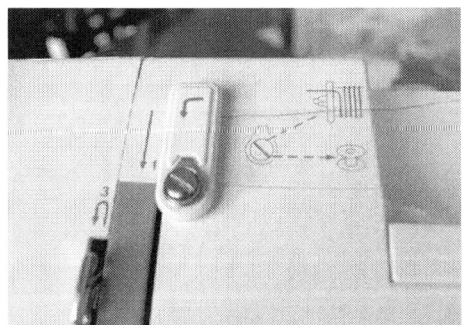

Begin by threading your machine with the coordinating shade of all-purpose thread to be used with your project. If you would like your stitching to be to not be seen opt for nylon monofilament for your top thread. Your machine will have a series of pictures from along the top that will guide you through threading your machine. Refer to the manual to make sure that this is done correctly.

2. Preparing your bobbin

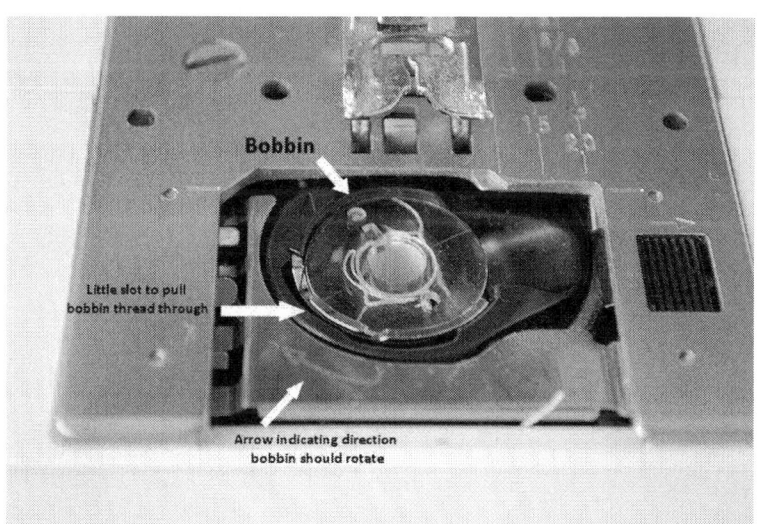

Bobbin

Little slot to pull bobbin thread through

Arrow indicating direction bobbin should rotate

Now that your machine is threaded, you will need to load your bobbin to match the backing fabric. The bobbin contains the bottom thread for your machine's stitch. However, you'll have to spin the thread on the bobbin before you can place it beneath the needle. You do this first by engaging the bobbin spinner on your machine.

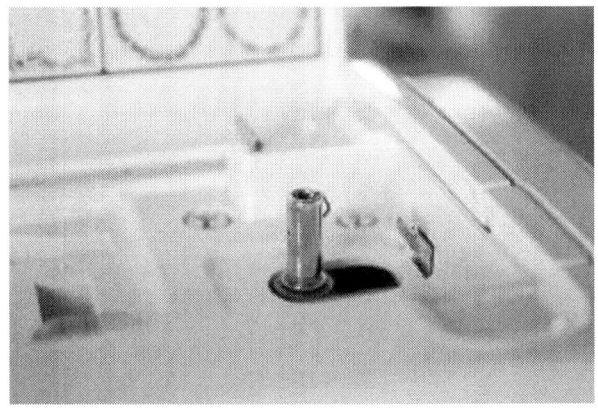

Usually, the bobbin spinner is engaged when it is pushed to the right. Once engaged, you'll attach the bobbin spool to the metal, and then pull the thread you want to be used as the bottom thread to wrap around the bobbin. You might want to hold the thread while the bobbin spins to make sure it won't come undone until it sets.

Start spinning the bobbin by pressing down on foot pedal. When the bobbin spinner is engaged, using the foot pedal will not engage the sewing machine needle. I like to start slow at first to make sure the thread wraps evenly around the bobbin spool. When I know that it has caught, I press down further to finish the job. When it's done, remove the bobbin and push the metal piece back to the left. Now pressing on the pedal will engage the sewing machine needle.

3. Change the stitch length

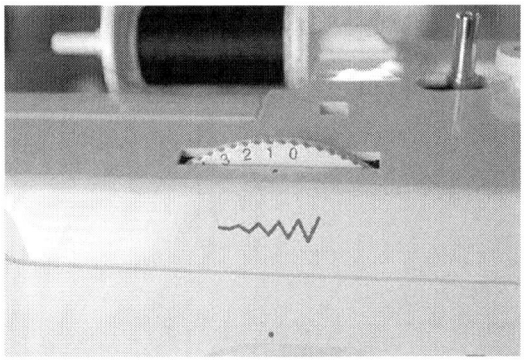

For machine quilting, you will want a stitch length between 6 and 10 stitches per inch. Follow the markings on your machine and set the wheel to adhere to these guidelines. Now you are ready to start stitching.

4. Make your first stitch

Place the center of the quilt in the machine and step on your pedal slowly to make one stitch only.

5. Pull the bottom stitch to the top

Keep the needle up from your previous stitch. Pull the top of the thread tail that is out so that your bobbin thread will come through the stitch that you made from the previous step. You should now have both of the thread tails from the top and bottom threads on top of the quilt.

6. Grab the two loops and pull through

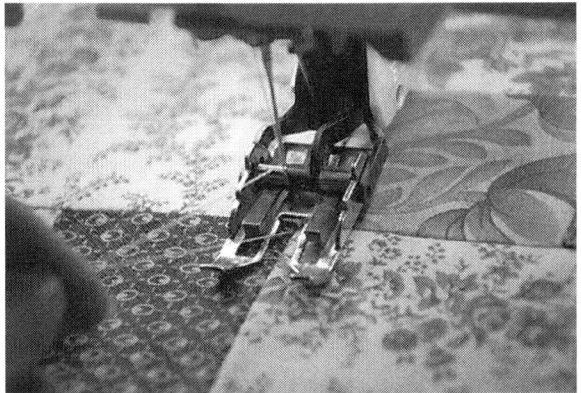

Hold these two different threads while you press on your pedal to make three or so stitches. Release the threads and engage your machine's back stitch function.

Back stitch for to the place where you first began. Your stitches are now knotted. Once you have knotted and secured your threading in place, you are now ready to begin stitching your quilt together.

7. Stitch normally

Place your foot on the pedal and stitch normally. Along the seams, pull out the pins as necessary. Stitch slowly so that your chances of mistakes are minimized.

8. Turn

When you reach a corner that requires turning in order to continue stitching, stop stitching with the needle lowered into the fabric. You can do this by taking your foot off the pedal, and using your machine manual wheel. Raise the pressure foot. Pivot the quilt in the direction you need to turn, and then lower the pressure foot onto the fabric again. Continue stitching.

10. Secure your stitching

When you reach a spot that requires you to stop stitching and knot your thread, take two stitches back in order to knot your thread, just as you did in step 6. With any type of sewing, you will be required to secure the thread at the beginning and the end every single time. If you do not do this, or forget this step, you risk your stitching coming undone. This can open your quilt causing unsightly holes in your finished product that you will need to repair manually later.

Once the open, unrolled area of your quilt is finished, remove the entire project from the machine to expose more of the quilt to be sewn. Place the project underneath the machine again as you did with the first step, and begin to quilt again. You will repeat this process until you have quilted the entire project.

References

1. http://www.generations-quilt-patterns.com/how-to-machine-quilt.html

2. http://www.generations-quilt-patterns.com/how-to-machine-quilt.html

3. http://www.generations-quilt-patterns.com/beginning-quilting.html

4. http://blog.shopmartingale.com/quilting-sewing/how-to-quilt-by-hand-for-beginners/

5. http://www.craftsy.com/blog/2013/07/basics-of-hand-quilting/

6. http://www2.fiskars.com/Sewing-Quilting/Projects/Tools-and-Techniques/Sewing-for-Beginners/How-to-Quilt#.VOgM33zF-So

7. http://www.threadsmagazine.com/item/3734/perfect-your-hand-quilting-stitch/page/all

About the Author

I started sewing years ago, when I was just a child and all I had was a needle and thread. I was turned onto making quilts for several years now and have simply fallen in love. I want to share that love with you and tell you everything you'll need to know (and more that's just good to know) to help you get started enjoying this love as well!

Manufactured by Amazon.ca
Bolton, ON